How is society possible?

Georg Simmel

© 2022 Culturea Editions
Illustration de couverture : © domaine public
Edition : Culturea, le patrimoine des lettres (Hérault, 34)
Contact : infos@culturea.fr
Retrouvez notre catalogue sur http://culturea.fr
Imprimé en Allemagne par Books on Demand
In de Tarpen 42, Norderstedt
Design typographique : Derek Murphy
Layout : Reedsy (https://reedsy.com/)
ISBN : 9791041941025
Dépôt légal : Décembre 2022

Georg Simmel

American Journal of Sociology, vol. 16 (1910-11)

Kant could propose and answer the fundamental question of his philosophy, How is nature possible?, only because for him nature was nothing but the representation (Vorstellung) of nature. This does not mean merely that "the world is my representation," that we thus can speak of nature only so far as it is a content of our consciousness, but that what we call nature is a special way in which our intellect assembles, orders, and forms the

sense-perceptions. These "given" perceptions, of color, taste, tone, temperature, resistance, smell, which in the accidental sequence of subjective experience course through our

consciousness, are in and of themselves not yet "nature;" but they become "nature" through the activity of the mind, which combines them into objects and series of objects, into substances and attributes and into causal coherences. As the elements of the world are given to us immediately, there does not exist among them, according to Kant, that coherence (Verbindung) which alone can make out of them the intelligible regular (gesetzmassig) unity of nature; or rather, which signifies precisely the being-nature (Natur-Sein) of those in themselves incoherently and irregularly emerging world-fragments. Thus the Kantian world-picture grows in the most peculiar reJection (Wiederspiel), Our sense-impressions are for this process purely subjective, since they depend upon the physico-psychical organization, which in other beings might be different, but they become "objects"

since they are taken up by the forms of our intellect, and by these are fashioned into fixed regularities and into a coherent picture of "nature." On the other hand, however, those perceptions are the real "given," the unalterably accumulating content of the world and the assurance of an existence independent of ourselves, so that now those very intellectual formings of the same into objects, coherences, regularities, appear as subjective, as that which is brought to the situation by ourselves, in contrast with that which we have received from the externally existent - i.e., these formings appear as the functions of the intellect itself, which in themselves unchangeable, had constructed from another sense-material a nature with another content. Nature is for Kant a definite sort of cognition, a picture growing through and in our cognitive categories. The question then, How is nature possible?, i.e., what are the conditions which must be present in order that a

"nature" may be given, is resolved by him through discovery of the forms which constitute the essence of our intellect and therewith bring into being "nature" as such.

It is at once suggested that it is possible to treat in an analogous fashion the question of the aprioristic conditions on the basis of which society - is possible. Here too individual elements are given which in a certain sense always remain in their discreteness, as is the case with the sense-perceptions, and they undergo their synthesis into the unity of a society only through a process of consciousness which puts the individual existence of the several elements into relationship with that of the others in definite forms and in accordance with definite laws. The decisive difference between the unity of a society and that of nature, however, is this: the latter - according to the Kantian standpoint here presupposed - comes to existence exclusively in the contemplating unity (Subject), it is produced exclusively by that mind upon and out of the sense materials which are not in themselves interconnected. On the contrary, the societary unity is realized by its elements without further mediation, and with no need of an observer, because these elements are consciously and synthetically active. The Kantian theorem, Connection (Verbindung) can never inhere in the things, since it is only brought into existence by the mind (Subject), is not true of the societary connection, which is rather immediately realized in the "things" - namely, in this case the individual souls. Moreover, this societary connection as synthesis, remains something purely psychical and without parallels with

space-structures and their reactions. But in the societary instance the combining requires no factor outside of its own elements, since each of these exercises the function which, with respect to the external, the psychic energy of the observer supplies. The consciousness of constituting with the others a unity is the whole unity in question in the societary case. This of course means, on the one hand, not the abstract consciousness of the unity concept, but the innumerable singular relationships, the feeling and knowing about this determining and being determined by the other, and, on the other hand, it quite as little excludes an observing third party from performing in addition a synthesis, with its basis only in himself, between the persons concerned, as between special elements. Whatever be the tract of externally observable being which is to be comprehended as a unity. the consummation occurs not merely by virtue of its immediate and strictly objective content, but it is determined by the categories of the mind (Subject) and from its cognitive requirements. Society, however, is the objective unity which has no need of the observer not contained in itself.

The things in nature are, on the one hand, more widely separated than souls. In the outward world, in which each entity occupies space which cannot be shared with another, there is no analogy for the unity of one man with another, which consists in understanding, in love, in common work. On the other hand, the fragments of spatial existence pass into a unity in the consciousness of the observer, which cannot be attained by community of individuals. For, on account of the fact that the objects of the societary synthesis are independent beings, psychic centres, personal unities, they resist that absolute merging in the soul of another person, to which the selflessness (Selbstlosigkeit) of soulless things must yield. Thus a collection of men is really a unity in a much higher, more ideal sense, yet in a much lower degree than tables, chairs, sofa, carpet and mirror constitute "the furniture of a room," or river, meadow, trees, house, "a landscape," or in a painting "a picture."

In quite a different sense from that in which it is true of the external world, is society "my representation" (

Vorstellung), i.e., posited upon the activity of consciousness.

For the soul of another has for me the same reality which I myself have, a reality which is very different from that of a material thing. However Kant insists that objects in space have precisely the same certainty as my own existence, in the latter case only the particular contents of my subjective life can be meant; for the basis of representation in general, the feeling of the existing ego, is unconditional and unshakable to a degree attained by no single representation of a material externality.

But this very certainty has for us, justifiably or not, also the fact of the thou; and as cause or as effect of this certainty we feel the thou as something independent of our representation, something which is just as really for itself (genau so fur sich ist) as our own existence. That this for-itself of the other nevertheless does not prevent us from making it into OUr representation, that something which cannot be resolved into our representing still becomes the content, and thus the product of our representation-this is the profoundest

psychologico-epistemological pattern and problem of

socialization. Within our own consciousness we distinguish very precisely between the fundamentality of the ego (the

presupposition of all representation, which has no part in the never wholly suppressible problematics of its contents) and these contents themselves, which as an aggregate, with their coming and going, their dubitability and their fallibility, always present themselves as mere products of that absolute and final energy and existence of our psychic being. We must carry over to the other soul, however, these very conditions, or rather independence of conditions, of our own ego, although in the last analysis we must represent that soul. That other soul has for us that last degree of reality which our own self possesses in distinction from its contents. We are sure that the case stands the same way with the other soul and its contents. Under these circumstances, the question, How is Society possible? has a wholly different methodological bearing from the question, How is nature possible?

The latter question is to be answered by the forms of cognition, through which the mind synthesizes given elements into "nature."

The former question is answered by the conditions residing a priori in the elements themselves, through which they combine themselves actually into the synthesis "society." In a certain sense the entire contents of this book, as developed on the basis of the principle announced, may be regarded as the material for answering this question. The book searches out the procedures, occurring in the last analysis in individuals, which condition the existence of the individuals as society. It does not treat these procedures as temporally antecedent causes of this result, but as partial processes of the synthesis which we

comprehensively name "society. "But the question must be understood in a still more fundamental sense. I said that the function of achieving the synthetic unity, which with reference to nature resides in the observing mind, with reference to society passes over to the societary elements themselves. The consciousness of constituting society is not to be sure, in the abstract, present in the individual; but everyone always knows that the others are connected with himself, although this knowing about the other as the associated, this recognizing of the whole complex as a society usually occurs with reference to particular concrete contents. Perhaps, however, the case is not different from that of "the unity of cognition" (die Einheit des Erkennens), according to which we proceed indeed in the processes of consciousness, arranging one concrete content with another, yet without having a separate consciousness of the unity itself, except in rare and late abstractions. Now, the question is: What lies then, universally and a priori at the basis, what presuppositions must be operative, in order that the particular concrete procedures in the individual consciousness may actually be processes of socialization; what elements are contained in them which make it possible that the product of the elements is, abstractly expressed, the construction of the individual into a societary unity? The sociological apriorities will have the same double significance as those "which make nature possible," on the one hand they will more or less completely determine the actual processes of socialization, as functions or energies of the psychical occurrence, on the other hand they are the ideal logical presuppositions of the perfect - although in this perfection never realized - society. A parallel is the use of the law of causation. On the one hand it lives and works in the actual cognitive processes. On the other hand it builds up the form of the truth as the ideal system of completed cognitions, irrespective of whether that truth is realized or not by that temporal, relatively accidental psychical dynamic, and irrespective of the greater or lesser approximation of the truth actually in consciousness to the ideal truth.

It is a mere question of terms whether investigation of these conditions of the socializing process shall be called

epistemological or not, since that structure which arises from these conditions, and which has its norms in their forms, is not cognitions but practical processes and real situations.

Nevertheless what I now have in mind, and what must be tested as the general concept of socialization by its conditions, is somewhat epistemological, viz., the consciousness of associating or of being socialized. Perhaps it should be called a knowing rather than a cognizing (besser ein Wissen als ein Erkennen). For in this case the mind does not immediately confront an object of which it gradually gains a theoretical picture, but that consciousness of the socialization is immediately its vehicle or inner significance. The matter in question is the processes of reciprocation which signify for the individual the fact of being associated. That is, the fact is not signified in the abstract to the individual, but it is capable of abstract expression. What forms must be at the basis, or what specific categories must we bring along, so to speak, in order that the consciousness may arise, and what consequently are the forms which the resulting consciousness - i.e., society as a fact of knowing - must bear?

We may call this the epistemological theory of society. In what follows, I am, trying to sketch certain of these a priori effective conditions or forms of socialization. These cannot, to be sure, like the Kantian categories, be designated by a single word. Moreover, I present them only as illustrations of the method of investigation.

1. The picture which one man gets of another from personal contact is determined by certain distortions which are not simple deceptions from incomplete experience, defective vision, sympathetic or antipathetic prejudice; they are rather changes in principle in the composition of the real object. These are, to begin with, of two dimensions. In the first place we see the other party in some degree generalized. This may be because it is not within our power fully to represent in ourselves an individuality different from our own. Every reconstruction (Nachbilden) of a soul is determined by the similarity to it, and although this is by no means the only condition of psychical cognition (sic) - since on the one hand unlikeness seems at the same time requisite, in order to gain perspective and

objectivity, on the other hand there is required an intellectual capacity which holds itself above likeness or unlikeness of being-yet complete cognition would nevertheless presuppose a complete likeness. It appears as though every man has in himself a deepest individuality-nucleus which cannot be subjectively reproduced by another whose deepest individuality is essentially different. And that this requirement is not logically compatible with that distance and objective judgment on which the representation of another otherwise rests, is proved by the mere fact that complete knowledge of the individuality of another is denied to us; and all interrelations of men with one another are limited by the varying degrees of this deficiency. Whatever its cause may be, its consequence at al events is a generalization of the psychical picture of the other person, a dissolving of the outlines, which adds to the singularity of this picture a relationship with others. We posit every man, with especial bearing upon our practical attitude toward him, as that type of man to which his individuality makes him belong. We think him, along with all his singularity, only under the universal category which does not fully cover him to be sure, and which he does not fully cover. This latter circumstance marks the contrast between this situation and that which exists between the universal idea and the particular which belongs under it. In order to recognize the man, we do not see him in his pure individuality, but carried, exalted or degraded by the general type under which we subsume him. Even when this transformation is so slight that we cannot immediately recognize it, or even if all the usual cardinal concepts of character fail us, such as moral or immoral, free or unfree, domineering or menial, etc. - in our own minds we designate the man according to an unnamed type with which his pure individuality does not precisely coincide.

Moreover this leads a step farther down. Precisely from the complete singularity of a personality we form a picture of it which is not identical with its reality, but still is not a general type. It is rather the picture which the person, would present if he were, so to speak, entirely himself, if on the good or bad side he realized the possibility which is in every man. We are all fragments, not only of the universal man, but also of ourselves. We are onsets not merely of the type human being in general, not merely of the type good, bad, etc., but we are onsets of that not further in principle nameable individuality and singularity of our own selves which surrounds our perceptible actuality as though drawn with ideal lines. The vision of our neighbor, however, enlarges this fragment to that which we never are completely and wholly. He cannot see the fragments merely side by side as they are actually given, but as we offset the blind spot in our eye so that we are not conscious of it, in like manner we make of these fragmentary data the completeness of an individuality. The practice of life is more and more insistent that we shall form our picture of the man from the real details alone which we empirically know about him; but this very practice rests upon those changes and additions, upon the reconstruction of those given fragments into the generality of a type and into the completeness of this ideal personality.

This procedure, which is in principle attempted, although in reality it is seldom carried through to completeness, operates only within the already existing society as the apriori of the further reactions which develop between individuals. Within a sphere which has any sort of community of calling or of interests, every member looks upon every other, not in a purely empirical way, but on the basis of an apriori which this sphere imposes upon each consciousness which has part in it. In the circles of officers, of church members, of civil officials, of scholars, of members of families, each regards the other under the matter of course presupposition-this is a member of my group.

From the common basis of life certain suppositions originate and people look upon one another through them as through a veil. This veil does not, to be sure, simply conceal the peculiarity of the individual, but it gives to this personality a new form, since its actual reality melts in this typical transformation into a composite picture. We see the other person not simply as an individual, but as colleague or comrade or fellow partisan; in a word, inhabitant of the same peculiar world; and this unavoidable, quite automatically operative presupposition is one of the means of bringing his personality and reality in the representation of another up to the quality and form demanded of his sociability (Soziabilitat).

The same is evidently true of members of different groups in their relations with one another. The plain citizen who makes the acquaintance of an officer cannot divest himself of the thought that this individual is an officer. And although this being an officer may belong to the given individuality, yet not in just the schematic way in which it prejudges his picture in the representation of the other person. The like is the case with the Protestant in contrast with the Catholic, the merchant with the official, the layman with the priest, etc. Everywhere there occur veilings of the outline of reality by the social generalization.

This in principle prohibits discovery of that reality within a group which is in a high degree socially differentiated.

Accordingly man's representation of man is thrown out of true by dislocations, additions and subtractions from all these categories, which exert an a priori influence, since the generalization is always at the same time more or less than the individuality. That is, the individual is rated as in some particulars different from his actual self by the gloss imposed upon him when he is classified in a type, when he is compared with an imagined completeness of his own peculiarity, when he is credited with the characteristics of the social generality to which he belongs. Over and above all this there sways, as the principle. of interpretation in cognition, the thought of his real solely individual equation; but since it appears as though determination of this equation would be the only way of arriving at the precisely founded relationship to the individual, as a matter of fact those changes and reshapings, which prevent this ideal recognition of him, are precisely the conditions through which the relationships which we know as the strictly social become possible - somewhat as with Kant the categories of reason, which form the immediately given into quite new objects, alone make the given world a knowable one.

2. Another category under which men (Subjecte) view

themselves and one another, in order that, so formed, they may produce empirical society, may be formulated in the seemingly trivial theorem: - Each element of a group is not a societary part, but beyond that something else. This fact operates as social apriori in so far as the part of the individual which is not turned toward the group, or is not dissolved in it, does not lie simply without meaning by the side of his socially significant phase, is not a something external to the group, for which it nolens volens affords space; but the fact that the individual, with respect to certain sides of his personality, is not an element of the group, constitutes the positive condition for the fact that he is such a group member in other aspects of his being. In other words, the sort of his socialized-being (Vergesellschaftet-Seins) is determined or partially determined by the sort of his not-socialized being. The analysis to follow will bring to light certain types whose sociological

significance, even in their germ and nature, is fixed by the fact that they are in some way shut out from the very group for which their existence is significant; for instance in the case of the stranger, the enemy, the criminal, and even the pauper. This applies, however, not merely in the case of such general characters, but in unnumbered modifications for every sort of individuality. That every moment finds us surrounded by relationships with human beings, and that the content of every moment's experience is directly or indirectly determined by these human beings, is no contradiction of the foregoing. On the contrary the social setting as such affects beings who are not completely bounded by it. For instance, we know that the civil official is not merely an official, the merchant not merely a merchant, the military officer not merely an officer. This extra-social being, his temperament and the deposit of his experiences, his interests and the worth of his personality, little as it may change the main matter of official, mercantile, military activities, gives the individual still, in every instance, for everyone with whom he is in contact, a definite shading, and interpenetrates his social picture with extra-social imponderabilities. The whole commerce of men within the societary categories would be different, if each confronted the other only in that character which belong; to him in the role for which he is responsible in the particular category in which he appears at the moment. To be sure, individuals, like callings and social situations, are distinguished by the degree of that In-addition which they possess or admit along with their social content. The man in love or in friendship may be taken as marking the one pole of this series. In this situation, that which the individual reserves for himself, beyond those manifestations and activities which converge upon the other, in quantity approaches the zero point. Only a single life is present, which, so to speak, may be regarded or is lived from two sides: on the one hand from the inside, from the terminus a quo of the active person; then on the other hand as the quite identical life, contemplated in the direction of the beloved person, under the category of gis terminus ad quem, which it completely adopts. With quite another tendency the Catholic priest presents in form the same phenomenon, in that his ecclesiastical function completely covers and swallows his being-for-himself. In the former of these extreme cases, the In-addition of the sociological activity disappears, because its content has completely passed over into consideration of the other party; in the second case, because the corresponding type of contents has in principle altogether disappeared. The opposite pole is exhibited by the phenomena of our modern civilization as they are determined by money economy.

That is, man approaches the ideal of absolute objectivity as producer, or purchaser or seller, in a word as a performer of some economic function. Certain individuals in high places excepted, the individual life, the tone of the total personality, has disappeared from the function, the persons are merely the vehicles of an exchange of function and counterfunction occurring according to objective norms, and every thing which does not fit into this sheer thingness (Sachlichkeit) has also as a matter of fact disappeared from it. The In-addition has fully taken up into itself the personality with its special coloring, its

irrationality, its inner life, and it has left to those societary activities only those energies, in pure abstraction, which specifically pertain to the activities.

Between these extremes the social individuals move in such a way that the energies and characteristics which are pointed toward the inner center always show a certain significance for the activities and inclinations which affect their associates.

For, in the marginal case, even the consciousness that this social activity or attitude is something differentiated from the rest of the man, and does not enter into the sociological relationship along with that which he otherwise is and signifies-even this consciousness has quite positive influence upon the attitude which the subject assumes towards his fellows and they towards him. The apriori of the empirical social life is that the life is not entirely social. We form our interrelationships not alone under the negative reservation of a part of our personality which does not enter into them; this portion affects the social occurrences in the soul not alone through general psychological combinations, but precisely the formal fact that influence exerts itself outside of these determines the nature of this interworking.

Still further, one of the most important sociological

formations rests on the fact that the societary structures are composed of beings who are at the same time inside and outside of them: namely that between a society and its individuals a relationship may exist like that between two parties-indeed that perhaps such relationship, open or latent, always exists.

Therewith society produces perhaps the most conscious, at least universal conformation of a basic type of life in general: that the individual soul can never have a position within a combination outside of which it does not at the same time have a position, that it cannot be inserted into an order without finding itself at the same time in opposition to that order. This applies throughout the whole range from the most transcendental and universal interdependencies to the most singular and accidental. The religious man feels himself completely encompassed by the divine being, as though he were merely a pulse-beat of the divine life; his own substance is unreservedly, and even in mystical identity, merged in that of the Absolute.

And yet, in order to give this intermelting any meaning at all, the devotee must retain some sort of self existence, some sort of personal reaction, a detached ego, to which the resolution into the divine All-Being is an endless task, a process only, which would be neither metaphysically possible nor religiously feelable if it did not proceed from a self-being on the part of the person: the being one with God is conditional in its significance upon the being other than god. Beyond this converging toward the transcendental, the relationship to nature as a whole which the human mind manifests throughout its entire history shows the same form. On the one hand we know ourselves as articulated into nature, as one of its products, which stands alongside of every other as an equal among equals, as a point which nature's stuff and energies reach and leave, as they circle through running water and blossoming plants. And yet the soul has a feeling of a something self-existent (eines Fursichseins) which we designate with the logically so inexact concept freedom, offering an opposite (ein Gegenuber und Paroli) to al that energy an element of which we ever remain, which makes toward the radicalism which we may express in the formula, Nature is only a representation in the human soul. As, however, in this conception, nature with il its undeniable peculiarity (Eigengesetzlichkeit) and hard reality is still subsumed under the concept of the ego, so on the other hand this ego, with all its freedom and self-containing (Fursichsein), with its juxtaposition to "mere nature," is still a member of nature. Precisely that is the overlapping natural correlation, that it embraces not ione "mere nature," but also that being which is independent and often enough hostile to "mere nature," that this which according to the ego's deepest feeling of selfishness is external to the ego must still be the element of the ego. Moreover, this formula holds not less for the relationship between the individuals and the particular circles of their societary combinations; or if we generalize these combinations into the concept of societary-ness in the abstract, for the interrelation of individuals at large. We know ourselves on the one side as products of society. The physiological series of progenitors, their adaptations and fixations, the traditions of their labor, their knowledge and belief, of the whole spirit of the past crystilized in objective forms-all these determine the equipment and the contents of our life, so that the question might arise whether the individual is anything more than a receptacle in which previously existing elements mix in changing proportions; for although the elements were also in the last analysis produced by individuals, yet the contribution of each is a disappearing quantity, and only through their generic and societary merging were the factors produced in the synthesis of which in turn the ostensible individuality may consist. On the other hand we know ourselves as a member of society, woven with our life-process and its meaning and purpose quite as

interdependently into its coexistence (Nebeneinander) as in the other view into its succession (Nacheinander). Little as we in our character as natural objects have a self-sufficiency, because the intersection of the natural elements proceeds through us as through completely selfless structures, and the equality before the laws of nature resolves our existence without remainder into a mere example of their necessity - quite as little do we live as societary beings around an autonomous center; but we are from moment to moment composed out of reciprocal relationships to others, and we are thus comparable with the corporeal substance which for us exists only as the sum of many impressions of the senses, but not as a self-sufficient entity. Now, however, we feel that this social diffusion does not completely dissolve our personality. This is not because of the reservations previously mentioned, or of particular contents whose meaning and development rest from the outset only in the individual soul, and finds no position at large in the social correlation. It is not only because of the molding of the social contents, whose unity as individual soul is not itself again of social nature, any more than the artistic form, in which the spots of color merge upon the canvas, can be derived from the chemical nature of the colors themselves. It is rather chiefly because the total life-content, however completely it may be applicable from the social antecedents and reciprocities, is yet at the same time capable of consideration under the category of the singular life, as experience of the individual and completely oriented with reference to this experience. The two, individual and experience, are merely different categories under which the same content falls, just as the same plant may be regarded now with reference to the biological conditions of its origin, again with reference to its practical utility, and still again with reference to its aesthetic meaning. The standpoint from which the existence of the individual may be correlated and understood may be assumed either within or without the individual; the totality of the life with all its socially derivable contents may be regarded as the centripetal destiny of its bearer, just as it still may pass, with all the parts reserved to the credit of the individual, as product and element of the social life.

Therewith, therefore, the fact of socialization bring; the individual into the double situation from which I started: viz., that the individual has his setting in the socialization and at the same time is in antithesis with it, a member of its organism and at the same time a closed organic whole, an existence (Sein) for it and an existence for itself. The essential thing, however, and the meaning of the particular sociological apriori which has its basis herein, is this, that between individual and society the Within and Without are not two determinations which exist alongside of each other - although they may occasionally develop in that way, and even to the degree of reciprocal enmity - but that they signify the whole unitary position of the socially living human being. His existence is not merely, in subdivision of the contents, partially social and partially individual, but it stands under the fundamental, formative, irreducible category of a unity, which we cannot otherwise express than through the synthesis or the contemporariness of the two logically antithetical determinations -articulation and self-sufficiency, the condition of being produced by, and contained in, society, and on the other hand, of being derived out of and moving around its own center. Society consists not only, as we saw above, of beings that in part are not socialized, but also of others that feel themselves to be, on the one hand, completely social existences, on the other hand, while maintaining the same content, completely individual existences. Moreover these are not two unrelated contiguous standpoints, as if, for instance, one considers the same body now with reference to its weight and now with reference to its color; but the two compose that unity which we call the social being, the synthetic category - as the concept of causation is an aprioristic unity, although it includes the two, in content, quite different elements of the causing and of the effect. That this formation is at our disposal, this ability to derive from beings, each of which may feel itself as the terminus a quo and as the terminus ad quem of its developments, destinies, qualities, the very concept of society which reckons with those elements, and to recognize the reality corresponding with the concept (Society) as the terminus a quo and the terminus ad quem of those vitalities and self-determinings - that is an apriori of empirical society, that makes its form possible as we know it.

3. Society is a structure of unlike elements. Even where democratic or socialistic movements plan an "equality," and partially attain it, the thing that is really in question is a like valuation of persons, of performances, of positions, while an equality of persons, in composition, in life-contents, and in fortunes cannot come into consideration. And where, on the other hand, an enslaved population constitutes only a mass, as in the great oriental despotisms, this equality of each always concerns only certain sides of existence, say the political or the economic, but never the whole of the same, the transmitted qualities, of which, personal relationships, experiences, not merely within the subjective aspect of life but also on the side of its reactions with other existences, will unavoidably have a certain sort of peculiarity and untransferability. If we posit society as a purely objective scheme, it appears as an

ordering of contents and performances which in space, time, concepts, values are concerned with one another, and as to which we may in so far peRform an abstraction from the personality, from the Ego-form, which is the vehicle of its dynamic. If that inequality of the elements now presents every performance or equality within this order as individually marked and in its place unequivocally established, at the same time society appears as a cosmos whose manifoldness in being and in movement is boundless, in which, however, each point can be composed and can develop itself only in that particular way, the structure is not to be changed. What has been asserted of the structure of the world in general, viz., that no grain of sand could have another form or place from that which now belongs to it, except upon the presupposition and with the consequence of a change of all being - the same recurs in the case of the structure of society regarded as a web of

qualitatively determined phenomena. An analogy as in the case of a miniature, greatly simplified and conventionalized

(stilisiert), is to be found for the picture of society thus conceived as a whole, in a body of officials, which as such consists of a definite ordering of "positions," of a pre-ordination of performances, which, detached from their personnel of a given moment, present an ideal correlation. Within the same, every newcomer finds an unequivocally assigned place, which has waited for him, as it were, and with which his energies must harmonize. That which in this case is a conscious, systematic assignment of functions, is in the totality of society of course an inextricable tangle of functions; the positions in it are not given by a constructive will, but they are discernible only through the actual doing and experiencing of individuals.

And in spite of this enormous difference, in spite of everything that is irrational, imperfect, and from the viewpoint of evaluation to be condemned, in historical society, its phenomenological structure - the sum and the relationship of the sort of existence and performances actually presented by all the elements of objectively historical society is an order of elements, each of which occupies an individually determined place, a coordination of functions and of functioning centers, which are objective and in their social significance full of meaning if not always full of value. At the same time, the purely personal aspect, the subjectively productive, the impulses and reflexes of the essential ego remain entirely out of

consideration. Or, otherwise expressed, the life of society runs its course-not psychologically, but phenomenologically, regarded purely with respect to its social contents - as though each element were predetermined for its place in this whole. In the case of every break in the harmony of the ideal demands, it runs as though all the members of this whole stood in a relation of unity, which relation, precisely because each member is his particular self, refers him to all the others and all the others to him.

From this point, then, the apriori is visible which should be now in question, and which signifies to the individual a foundation and a "possibility" of belonging to a society. That each individual, by virtue of his own quality, is automatically referred to a determined position within his social milieu, that this position ideally belonging to him is also actually present in the social whole - this is the presupposition from which, as a basis, the individual leads his societary life, and which we may characterize as the universal value of the individuality. It is independent of the fact that it works itself up toward clear conceptional consciousness, but also of the contingent possibility of finding realization in the actual course of life -

as the apriority of the law of causation, as one of the normative preconditions of all cognition, is independent of whether the consciousness formulates it in detached concepts, and whether the psychological reality always proceeds in accordance with it or not. Our cognitive life rests on the presupposition of a pre-established harmony between our spiritual energies, even the most individual of them, and external objective existence, for the latter remains always the expression of the immediate phenomenon, whether or not it can be traced back metaphysically or psychologically to the production of the reality by the intellect itself. Thus societary life as such is posited upon the presupposition of a fundamental harmony between the individual and the social whole, little as this hinders the crass dissonances of the ethical and the eudaemonistic life. If the social reality were unrestrictedly and infallibly given by this preconditional principle, we should have the perfect society -

again not in the sense of ethical or eudaemonistic but of conceptual perfection. More fully expressed, we should have, so to speak, not the perfect society, but the perfect society. So far as the individual finds, or does not find, realization of this apriori of his social existence, i.e., the thoroughgoing correlation of his individual being with the surrounding circles, the integrating necessity of his particularity, determined by his subjective personal life, for the life of the whole, the socialization is incomplete; the society has stopped short of being that gapless reciprocality which its concept foretells.

This state of the case comes to a definite focus with the category of the vocation (Beruf). Antiquity, to be sure, did not know this concept in the sense of personal differentiation and of the society articulated by division of labor.

But what is at the basis of this conception was in existence even in antiquity; viz., that the socially operative doing is the unified expression of the subjective qualification, that the whole and the permanent of the subjectivity practically objectifies itself by virtue of its functions in the society.

This relationship was realized then on the average merely in a less highly differentiated content. Its principle emerged in the Aristotelian dictum that some were destined by their nature to

[Greek word omitted], others to [Greek word omitted]. With higher development of the concept it shows the peculiar structure - that on the one hand the society begets and offers in itself a position (Stelle) which in content and outline differs from others, which, however, in principle may be filled out by many, and thereby is, so to speak, something anonymous; and that this position now, in spite of its character of generality, is grasped by the individual, on the ground of an inner "call," or of a qualification conceived as wholly personal. In order that a

"calling" may be given, there must be present, however it came to exist, that harmony between the structure and the life-process of the society on the one side, and the individual make-up and impulses on the other. Upon this as general precondition rests at last the representation that for every personality a position and a function exists within the society, to which the personality is

"called," and the imperative to search until it is found.

The empirical society becomes "possible" only through the apriori which culminates in the "vocation" concept, which apriori to be sure, like those previously discussed, cannot be characterized by a simple phrase, as in the case of the Kantian categories. The consciousness processes wherewith socialization takes place - unity composed of many, the reciprocal

determination of the individuals, the reciprocal significance of the individual for the totality of the other individuals and of the totality for the individual - run their course under this precondition which is wholly a matter of principle, which is not recognized in the abstract, but expresses itself in the reality of practice: viz., that the individuality of the individual finds a position in the structure of the generality, and still more that this structure in a certain degree, in spite of the incalculability of the individuality, depends antecedently upon it and its function. The causal interdependence which weaves each social element into the being and doing of every other, and thus brings into existence the external network of society, is transformed into a teleological interdependence, so soon as it is considered from the side of its individual bearers, its producers, who feel themselves to be egos, and whose attitude grows out of the soil of the personality which is self-existing and self-determining. That a phenomenal wholeness of such character accommodates itself to the purpose of these

individualities which approach it from without, so to speak, that it offers a station for their subjectively determined

life-process, at which point the peculiarity of the same becomes a necessary member in the life of the whole - this, as a fundamental category, gives to the consciousness of the individual the form which distinguishes the individual as a social element!

Lightning Source UK Ltd.
Milton Keynes UK
UKHW010712301222
414627UK00004B/403

9 791041 941025